MW01487256

12 PILLARS

OF PEAK PERFORMANCE

*A STORY ABOUT BECOMING
A PEAK PERFORMER*

*Book #1 in
The 12 Pillars of Peak Performance Book Series*

BRIAN CAIN

Brian Cain Peak Performance, LLC

"Brian Cain is a 21st-century version of King Midas. Everything he touches doesn't turn to gold, but the ideas he shares in this book are pure gold. This is the best book I have ever read."

Todd Whitting
Head Baseball Coach
The University of Houston

"We have used *The 12 Pillars of Peak Performance* in our program at LSU and the results have showed up on the field. This is more than a book. It's a road map for success in athletics and in life."

Beth Torina
Head Softball Coach
Louisiana State University

"*The 12 Pillars of Peak Performance* is at the core of our program at TCU. This book with show you the path to success."

Jim Schlossnagle
Head Baseball Coach
TCU

"We have implemented *The 12 Pillars of Peak Performance* on and off the field at Yale. This blueprint is the backbone of our program."

Tony Reno
Head Football Coach
Yale University

"Brian Cain has helped us create a championship culture at Fuddruckers. Everyone in our organization will read this book and love it."

Luke Mandola, Jr.
Senior Vice President
Fuddruckers

"This is one of the easiest and most informative books I have ever read. *The 12 Pillars of Peak Performance* is a lifestyle that you will want to live after reading this book."

Wade Anderson
Director of Sales
Paul Mitchell

"Simple, powerful, riveting. I laughed, I cried and I am inspired to take massive action after reading this. I can't wait to see what happens next."

John Brubaker
Author of Seeds of Success

"Truly a fun book that we will use with our team every year and talk about every day."

Raegan Pebley
Head Women's Basketball Coach
Texas Christian University

Brian M. Cain, MS, CMAA
Mental Conditioning Coach
Peak Performance Publishing
Brian Cain Peak Performance, LLC

The 12 Pillars of Peak Performance

A Masters of the Mental Game Series Book

©2016 by Brian M. Cain, MS, CMAA

Printed in the United States of America
Edited by: Mary Lou Schueler

ISBN 10: 1523400935
ISBN 13: 978-1523400935

THE 12 PILLARS OF PEAK PERFORMANCE

A Story about Becoming a Peak Performer

INTRODUCTION

Matthew Simonds is a well-respected and highly sought-after business consultant who has reached a pivotal crossroads in his life. Spending 280 days a year on the road is taking its toll on his health and on the relationship with his wife and kids.

He is on his way home from consulting in Detroit to celebrate Thanksgiving and his wife's birthday with the family when his travel plans get interrupted unexpectedly and puts him into a tailspin of negativity where he just can't take it anymore.

Coach Kenny, a former Olympic athlete and current sport psychologist to some of the greatest coaches, athletes, musicians, actors and corporate executives in the world, invites Matthew Simonds to get a checkup from the neck up, stop feeling sorry for himself, and start living a life by design by following his optimal system of living, The 12 Pillars of Peak Performance.

Coach Kenny and Matthew Simonds take you on a journey into the soul of a man and the system of success that has helped create champions in all aspects of performance.

The system that has helped Coach Kenny and his team will serve Matthew Simonds in his pursuit of becoming more, and it will serve you in yours.

CHAPTER 1

The
Tarmac

I couldn't wait to get home. I had been on the road for 13 straight days and was so fired up to get home to see my beloved wife Erin, daughter Brina and son Michael. I knew that if I could just make it through this week, I would be home for Thanksgiving and her birthday and would be able to invest the time into my family that I wanted to but had been unable to because of being too busy at work.

Then what I hoped and prayed wouldn't happen did.

"Ladies and gentlemen, this is your captain speaking. We are having some mechanical issues and are going to have to return to the terminal."

My heart sank. Another delay. As I sat there, I muttered to myself, "You have to be kidding me."

The old man sitting next to me, who I thought was sleeping, opened his eyes, looked over at me and said, "I'm sorry. What did you say, son?"

"Nothing. I was just talking to myself."

"Well, I thought you were complaining that we were going back to the terminal," he said. "I'm just glad we didn't take off. The last thing you want is for the captain to diagnose a mechanical issue once you have taken off – then none of us are getting home. Better late and alive than never, I always say."

"That's a great point. I just wish I could get home on time once in my life," I said.

"Home? Home is where your feet are and right now you are on this plane, so you might as well enjoy it 'cause from the looks of it, we are going to be here a while," the man said. "My name is Ken. My friends call me Coach Kenny. What's yours?"

"I am Matthew, Matthew Simonds," I said.

"Well, Matthew Simonds, it's nice to meet you. I am on my way home too. I live in Southlake, Texas. Was here in Detroit seeing some of my friends."

"Coach Kenny, did you say you live in Southlake, Texas? So do I. Small world," I said. "Did you say your sons are in Detroit?"

"Yes. I work as a sport psychology coach and

although the coaches and athletes I am working with up here are my clients, I consider them my friends and teammates and treat them like my sons and daughters. I think of them like that so that I can be my best for them," Coach Kenny said. "What brings you up here, Matthew Simonds?"

"My job," I said with a sigh. "I work as a business consultant and I was up here seeing some clients and putting out some fires. Nothing too exciting actually."

"That's too bad that you don't find what you do to be exciting. You only get one chance at this game called life, and one of the keys to victory is to find what you love and do it every day. When you do that, you will never work a day in your life," Coach Kenny said. "After the Olympics in 1960 I went to work as a sport psychology coach and have never worked a day in my life – I love it. I want to do it. It keeps me up at night and kicks me out of bed in the morning just like training for the Olympics used to. Now at 80, I can't move as well as I used to, but my mental game is better than ever."

I had no idea I was sitting next to an Olympic

athlete. My wife was an Olympic Ice Hockey player and I had always been fascinated with the dedication and commitment that she made to her training and to her mindset.

"Coach Kenny, you still look like you should be competing," I said. He was in great shape for any age. For 80, he was an absolute specimen. "That's awesome that you were an Olympian. What sport did you do?"

"I did the decathlon. You know, the one where you do four runs, three jumps and three throws and you get crowned as the best athlete in the world if you win," he said. "Well, I never won a medal, but the lessons I learned in training and the lessons I learned since the Olympics have been worth more to me than any medal would have been. Don't get me wrong; I love to win. I just love to learn more. You see, Matthew Simonds, in life there are winners and... what do you think? Winners and..."

"Losers," I said.

"NO!" He said with an energy and passion I had not seen in a long time. "There are winners and learners in life, and the biggest gold medals of them all go around the necks of those who learn the most. You are either learning or you are getting left behind. You are either learning and growing or you are staying the same and dying. And it looks like you have a whole lot of learning to do, Matthew Simonds. How much do you travel for work?"

"About 280 days a year I said."

"280 days a year on the road, and you are married with kids?" Coach Kenny asked as he leaned in to get closer. "You won't be married for long in my opinion if you keep it up. Proximity is power in any relationship and if you are on the road that much, it sounds like you are living to work instead of working to live?"

Coach Kenny was right. I was treading on thin ice. I had let myself go physically, I had not been as present with Erin, Brina and Michael as I wanted to be, and I had not been home much at all. The money was good, but the lifestyle and the travel were killing me.

I wondered how Coach Kenny could know so much about me so fast sitting here on the tarmac? Was this guy a wizard or was I really wearing my life on my sleeve that easily for people to see? I thought that if he could see it, so could my clients and maybe that was part of why I had been underperforming lately.

When we got to the terminal, passengers started getting up and heading back inside. As I took my phone out of my pocket to text Erin that I was delayed again, I sat there numb, taking to heart what Coach Kenny had said about winners and learners, about either growing or dying, about not working a day in your life when you loved what you did, about proximity being power and living to work vs. working to live. I used to love what I did, but I think I lost some of that love.

As I finished sending a text to Erin, I looked up and he was gone. I was one of the last ones on the plane. I got up and started to walk back into the airport, hoping that they would get the plane to fly.

I just wanted to get home.

CHAPTER 2

The
Next Flight

When I got to the top of the jet bridge and walked in the airport, the line at the National Airlines ticket counter looked like a line of people waiting to get into a Motley Crue concert – it was packed. My flight from Detroit to Dallas wasn't the only one that had been delayed.

Rather than wait in line to find out what was going to happen, I called the National Airlines customer service center. After waiting for almost 20 minutes, an operator picked up the phone and said she had good news and bad news. The good news was that due to the mechanical issue with the plane, I had automatically been booked on the next available flight back to Dallas. The bad news was that flight wasn't until Saturday morning.

"Saturday morning," I said with a rage of frustration. "It's Wednesday, Thanksgiving is tomorrow, and my wife's birthday is on Friday. I have to get home today."

"I'm sorry, Mr. Simonds. This is a busy time of year for travelers, you know, and that flight on Saturday is our next available seat," said the agent. "I checked with our partner airlines and they don't have any available seats either. Now, my records show that they have not officially canceled your original flight yet, so I'd stay by the gate and keep your fingers crossed."

CHAPTER 3

The
Voice

As I made my way to find a seat at our gate in hopes of a status update on our flight, I heard a familiar voice.

"Matthew, Matthew Simonds. Over here, son."

As I looked to my left, there was Coach Kenny sitting at a table inside the airport Fuddruckers with a burger and a beverage.

"Come on in, son. We are going to be here a while. Might as well take a load off and fuel the machine," he said.

I thought to myself, *What the heck. I am going to be here a while. I might as well sit with the old man and have myself one of the world's greatest hamburgers.*

I went in, sat down and ordered my favorite Fuddruckers burger – a 2/3rd pound burger with Swiss cheese, mushrooms, grilled onions and avocados. I got myself a cold beverage as well and took a deep breath as I sat back in my chair, wondering how I was going to get home.

"We can't control the airline, the plane, the pilot and a whole heck of a lot of other things, so we might as well enjoy what we can control, which is some great food," Coach Kenny said with a smile. "Now if I remember right, Matthew Simonds, did you say you were on the road 280 days a year?"

"Yes, about 220 too many," I said. "I set a goal a long time ago to reach a level of financial security by the time I was 40. I wanted to have my house in Southlake paid off, a strong security cushion in savings, and enough in my investments where I could draw about $5K a month in interest and live off that so I could be home more and basically retire. It's been a lofty goal and one I have been relentlessly pursuing for years now. A lot of times I wonder if the cost of pursuing that goal is worth it?"

"Damn, son, that's a big goal for someone as young as you," Coach Kenny said. "But that's what life is all about, setting and getting big goals. Setting big goals is great, but they have to be the right goals or they become traps. Financial goals must be secondary to family goals or you won't have any family to set goals with."

I sat for a minute and thought. Coach Kenny was right. I had set this financial goal before I had gotten married and had kids and it was still my

#1 goal. I was putting finance over family and it was costing me more than any amount of money was worth. I couldn't even remember the last time I had kissed my wife, and the last thing my son Michael had said when I was walking out the door while on the phone was, "Daddy, why do you love your cell phone more than me?" My heart sank as my wife looked at me and said, "I was starting to wonder the same thing." It was like a one-two combination right to the gut.

"You make a lot of good points, Coach Kenny," I said. "I feel like you know me and we just met. Am I that easy to read?"

"Look, as humans we all wear our emotions somewhere," Coach Kenny said. "Some of us more than others. With you, I am able to see your stress in your breathing on the plane, your body language in the way you were walking in the airport and in how you are sitting right now. It's easy for me to see, but probably not as easy for others who are not as cued in on emotional intelligence as I am, and probably impossible for you to see in yourself. We are often the last to see in ourselves what everyone else sees. The only way to speed up that process is to have two things."

"What two things? A burger and a beverage?" I chuckled.

"That helps," Coach Kenny laughed. "No, what you need are..."

"Attention, Passengers on National Airlines Flight 4824 from Detroit to Dallas," the woman's voice said over the PA system as we both sat up straight and listened. "This flight has been canceled due to a mechanical issue. Please see an agent for rebooking on the next available flight."

My heart sank. I wasn't getting home anytime soon.

CHAPTER 4

The
Two Things

"That sucks!" I yelled as slammed my fists on the table in another rage of frustration. Not only was I not going to get home for Thanksgiving I was also going to miss Erin's birthday.

"What are you going to do about it?" Coach Kenny asked? "Are you going to sit here and continue to feel sorry for yourself or are you going to see if you can get on that next plane? Feeling sorry for yourself never did anyone any good and it won't serve well in this instance either. It's worthless, useless emotion. Take a deep breath and enjoy your burger."

I took a deep breath, sighed, and again said, "That's a good point. You seem to be making a lot of those tonight."

"Look, you can focus on what is or you can focus on what if," Coach Kenny said. "If you focus on 'what if,' your mind plays tricks on you and you get lost because you get too far into the future. If you play the 'what is' game, you start to feel better because you can actually do something about what is and improve your situation."

"I called in earlier. The next seat they have on a plane back to Dallas isn't until Saturday," I said. "I am going to miss Thanksgiving with the kids and my wife's birthday. She is going to be pissed. She told me not to come on this one trip because of the holiday and how a few years ago I got stuck in Vermont and couldn't get home for Thanksgiving. I told her that's because it was Vermont and that the Detroit airport was much bigger and that delays never happen in Detroit. She is going to be pissed."

"And she is going to be right," Coach Kenny said. "If you had the option to go home earlier and didn't, your actions clearly show you value finance over family. You need the two things we were talking about before they made that announcement. These are the two things every great athlete has. Do you want to know what they are?"

"Yes sir," I said.

"You need a coach and an accountability partner. A coach to train you on the 12 Pillars of Peak Performance so that you can live a life of excellence and fulfillment in all areas of your life, and an accountability partner to help you stay on course and on target so that you don't drift so far to one side that you get lost," Coach Kenny said.

"Right now it seems like you have drifted too far to the financial side and are losing your family because of it."

Coach Kenny was right. I served as a coach and accountability partner for people in my job, and didn't have either a coach or accountability partner for myself in my own life. I was not practicing what I teach and it was costing me.

I wondered if Coach Kenny would be my coach and accountability partner. Before I was going to ask him about that, I knew I had to call home first so I could explain to Erin why I wasn't going to be home. This was one phone call I didn't want to make.

As I stood up from the table and walked over to the side of the restaurant for some privacy, my palms started to sweat and my heart sank as I reached into my pocket for the phone.

CHAPTER 5

The Phone Call

"Saturday! You can't get home till Saturday? I hate to tell you I told you so. But, I told you so. I knew this was going to happen. I knew you would get stuck, Matthew. Thanks for missing Thanksgiving and my birthday... again!"

Those were exactly the words I was expecting to hear from Erin. She had a funny way of predicting what was going to happen. She was always talking about The Law of Attraction and how TBT – Thoughts Become Things – and that you attract to you what you think about most often. I was thinking a lot about how bad it would be if my flight got delayed and how terrible it would be if I didn't make it home. Ironic. That's exactly what happened.

"What am I supposed to tell Michael and Brina? Dad won't be home for Thanksgiving because he wants to work more than be with you?" Erin said as she fought back tears. "They already hardly know you because you are never home. They probably won't know any different anyway. Can't you get in a car and drive home? Isn't there another flight? You always say that you can find a way or you can find an excuse but you can't do both. Time to start living what you teach, Matthew."

As she hung up the phone I could feel the sadness, disappointment and frustration in her voice. I couldn't blame her. I didn't HAVE to come to Detroit; I chose to.

Erin always says that when you say *yes* to one thing you say *no* to something else. She always challenged me to be aware of what I was saying *yes* to because I seemed to always say *no* to her and the kids. I knew I needed to start saying *no* to others so that I could say *yes* to them.

When I got back to the table, Coach Kenny was staring at his phone with a smile a mile wide.

I sat down, put my head into my hands and thought about how I was going to get home.

"I love you to my sweet honeysuckle," Coach Kenny said.

I sat up and looked at Coach Kenny, wondering if he was speaking to me. Then he leaned over and kissed his phone.

"See you when I see you, but know you are always in my vision. Dominate the day, baby. I love you."

He then hung up the phone and reached for a French fry on his plate.

"Did you just kiss your phone?" I asked him, laughing.

"Sure did. Do it every night that I don't get to do it in person," Coach Kenny said. "Whenever I am on the road, I will send a morning selfie video wishing my wife Brittany a blessed day and then at night we FTK, which stands for FaceTime Kiss, and I tell her how much I love her. This is a key part of our routine, and no matter how many days I am away, it's never too long when you get that FaceTime kiss each night. Don't get me wrong; nothing is as good as the real thing."

FaceTime kiss, morning selfie videos. This guy was a stud. Why had I not thought of that? That seemed so simple, so easy to do. A great way for me to stay connected to Erin and the kids when I was on the road.

As I sat back in my chair, I looked across the table at a man who I felt could really help me.

I just needed to work up the courage to ask him four help.

CHAPTER 6

The Five
Magic Words

"Coach Kenny. Can you help me?" I asked with the look of a man who was beaten down by life and feeling lost. "I know I just met you and all, but I feel like I could learn a lot from you. I feel like I am losing, and I need your help. Are you taking on any new clients?"

Coach Kenny sat up straight and took a sip of his beverage. He leaned across the table and looked me straight in the eye with the focused stare that only an Olympic athlete could muster.

"Did you say you felt like a loser? Son, did you not hear what I said earlier about there being no such thing as a loser?" Coach Kenny asked. "In life there are winners and learners. I can't help you if you are not willing to listen, and you can't help yourself if you are not willing to ask for help. Asking for help is a sign of strength, a sign of humble confidence. The humility to know you don't have all the answers and the confidence to know that you are working to get better – and the most important thing anyone can do is have a rage for mastery, a passion for getting better, for learning and applying what you learn.

"Unfortunately, I'm not taking any new clients. However, if you allow me to buy you this dinner, I will share with you the philosophy and system that I learned while training to be an Olympian, which is the same system I use to train the people I work with to give themselves the best chance for success," Coach Kenny said. "I call it the 12 Pillars of Peak Performance. I will work with you only if you are willing to listen and to apply. I don't have time for clients that don't listen, don't apply and don't make time for themselves."

"Coach Kenny, I will listen and I will apply. Thank you so very much," I said. "I have been thinking about what you said, about needing a coach and an accountability partner. I do that for other people; I just don't do it for myself. I will do what you coach me to do if you think it will help me get to where I want to be."

Coach Kenny then asked me one of the most difficult questions in the world.

"Let me ask you the five magic words Matthew Simonds, What do you really want? We need to start there. What do you really want?"

As I took a deep breath, I realized that I had not been asking myself one of the most important questions that I ask my clients. I always started out my coaching sessions in the corporate world by asking my clients what they really wanted. I guess I never asked myself that same thing.

Now, more than ever, I needed to.

CHAPTER 7

What Do You Really Want?

"You must get clear on what you really want and you must get clear on how you define success for yourself. Otherwise you are playing on someone else's scoreboard vs. your scoreboard that you intentionally set," Coach Kenny said. "Success is not what society wants you to think. It has nothing to do with the size of your house, the size of your bank account, the type of car you drive or the amount of places you have been for vacation. Success is purely to be measured by the individual and how that individual lives compared to the vision he holds of his best self. So again, Matthew Simonds, what do you really want, and how do you define success for yourself?"

I sat in silence. I had lost my vision for what I really wanted. I had no measurements for success. I was going through life on a mission to achieve my goal of financial security and I was risking what was most important to me – my family – in the process. I was also in the worst shape of my life at 240lbs and felt like I was lost in so many areas of life.

"I don't know what I really want, Coach Kenny," I said dejectedly. "I thought I wanted to achieve a level of financial security, and I have let that goal consume me. I am losing my health and the ones I love in pursuit of that goal and it's not worth it."

Coach Kenny then said something that hit me right between the eyes.

"Be careful of who you become in pursuit of what you want."

I thought about that for a minute. It was so profound. I was becoming a man I didn't want to be because of the pursuit of a goal. I ate, drank and gambled too much, and didn't exercise enough or spend enough time with my wife and kids. I was so busy trying to please and serve those outside of my house that I was sacrificing and neglecting those I cared about most. I was letting myself go vs. taking care of my family and working to be the best I could be in all areas.

"Again, Matthew Simonds. What do you really want?"

As I took a bite of my burger and a sip of my beverage to buy some time, it hit me.

"What I really want is to be significant in the lives of my wife and kids, to be a great husband and father, to be significant in the lives of others and to do what I love to do, which is help coach and teach others to live a life of excellence and fulfillment."

Coach Kenny then handed me his cell phone and had me text what I really wanted to myself so that we both had it on our phones. It's crazy to think, but as I sent that text, it felt kind of like a weight was being lifted off my back.

"That's a great start, Matthew Simonds, and it's the start that stops most people," Coach Kenny said. "Now what we need to do is equip you with a toolbox and plan to help you grow into the type of person that can be significant in the lives of his wife and kids, be a great husband and father, be significant in the lives of others and who gets to do what he loves to do, which is help coach and teach others to live a life of excellence and fulfillment.

"The start is to chart your destination. Now we must go to work on giving you the skills you need to be the best you can be to navigate the course. Remember, if you influence and impact others, you will make an income. You have focused on income first, and when you do that, you actually make less income because you lose focus on the influence and impact you have on others," Coach Kenny said.

"We are going to focus on the best ways you can have influence and impact on others by starting with yourself. Remember, those who you lead, both in your house and in your coaching, need a model to see and they need a motto to say," Coach Kenny said. "My experience says that people need both a model and a motto, and the model always comes first. We are going to coach you on how to be the model for others to see in line with the vision for your future, and we're going to do that by taking you through my signature training system."

CHAPTER 8

The 12 Pillars of Peak Performance

I wanted to be a model for others to see, a leader for others to look to. I knew I was falling short in a lot of areas, especially in my own home. What Coach Kenny said made so much sense to me in such a short period of time. I was fired up to learn about his signature training system.

At the same time, I was torn. I felt like I should go get a rental car and start driving the 17.5 hours it would take to get back home, or at least start the trip by checking into a hotel and getting some sleep, and then start the drive in the morning.

But I wanted more. Coach Kenny spoke in a way that resonated with me like my high school football coach John Allen.

Coach Allen was one of the first people to believe in me and to teach about the importance of the mental game. I had lost contact with Coach Allen, but never lost contact with his teachings.

"Matthew Simonds, the 12 Pillars of Peak Performance have been around forever. They are used and taught by the greatest achievers of all time. Not one person excels in all 12 of the Pillars, yet I have seen a direct correlation with the success of an individual or a group and their commitment to growing in each of the 12 Pillars," Coach Kenny said. "Growth is the key. Growth is the first step to mastery. If you keep growing, you will master. Let's start with Pillar #1, because I already know you need it."

CHAPTER 9

Pillar #1
Elite Mindset

"Pillar #1 is understanding that you train an elite mindset just like you train your body or any other physical skill that you would use in sport or in business. The ideal way to train anything is through a total immersion experience followed by spaced repetition, and that spaced repetition is called doing a little a lot, not a lot a little," Coach Kenny said. "Whether it was training for the Olympics years ago or the work I currently do with top athletes and corporate executives, the total immersion, shock-your-system approach followed by spaced repetitious follow-up and a behavioral and goal accountability partner is ideal.

"An elite mindset is a mindset in which you are able to think the same way as the best of the best, which leads to a performance like the best of the best," Coach Kenny stated. "Let's look at some of the fundamental differences in thinking between average and elite.

"People with an average mindset use the phrase *have to*; people with an elite mindset use the words *get to or want to*.

"People with an average mindset focus on how they feel. People with an elite mindset focus on how they act and what they need to do, not how they feel about doing it. Don't let feelings drive you; let your actions drive you.

"People with an average mindset make an excuse, but people with an elite mindset make it happen.

"People with an average mindset feel sorry for themselves; people with an elite mindset are so focused on others that they do not have time to feel sorry for themselves and know that feeling sorry for yourself is a worthless and useless emotion.

"People with an average mindset say it's impossible; people with an elite mindset say it's going to be very difficult.

"People with an average mindset see a failure as final, while people with an elite mindset see failure as positive feedback and every setback as a setup for a comeback.

"People with an average mindset wear their emotions on their sleeves; people with an elite mindset never show weakness and are always

BIG with their body language so they can be the rock of confidence for others.

"People with an average mindset see confidence as a feeling, but people with an elite mindset know that confidence is an action.

"People with an average mindset focus on what they can't control; people with an elite mindset focus on what they can control."

By this point I had taken my phone out of my pocket, flipped it on airplane mode and turned on the voice memos app to record the golden nuggets of wisdom that Coach Kenny was sharing. I also started scribbling down on a napkin as fast as I could the most important ideas he was sharing.

"Coach Kenny, this is great stuff. How did you learn to think this way and build such a great perspective?" I asked.

"I didn't always think like this," Coach Kenny replied. "There are two primary mindsets: a growth and a fixed mindset. For a long time I had a fixed mindset and thought that was the way I was and that was it. When I got around some of the other athletes training for the Olympics, I changed. I was physically gifted, but mentally I was behind. Being around the other athletes and some really good coaches opened up my eyes to a new way of thinking, and a growth mindset emerged.

"Now I try to read a book a week and put in to action what I learn. I just can't get enough. I wish I had taken this approach to learning when I was your age. I know I don't have a lot of time left to live, but I am going to learn like I will live forever. I am going to live a lot in the time I do have left and I am going to give away as much as I can. I can't take anything up here with me to the grave so I might as well give it all away," Coach Kenny said as he pointed to his head.

I thought about how elite of a mindset he must have and how much more to this new way of thinking there must be. I related more to examples of the people with an average mindset than I did to the people with an elite mindset and I wanted to change. I wanted to grow my elite mindset.

"Having an elite mindset is great. But it's not enough," Coach Kenny said. "Having an elite mindset is like having a $100,000 sports car in your garage. When you look at it, it's amazing. It sounds impressive when you rev the engine. The only problem is that if you don't put tires on that car, it's not going to take you anywhere.

"The tires are your MVP Process. And your MVP Process is everything," Coach Kenny said.

I was a little confused. What did he mean, *your MVP Process?*

-Turn have to into want to or get to

-Focus on how you act over how you feel

-Make it happen, not an excuse

-Never feel sorry for yourself

-Nothing is impossible, it's just difficult

-Failure is positive feedback

-Never show weakness, be strong.

-Your MVP Process is everything

CHAPTER 10

Pillar #2 Championship Culture

"The MVP is your mission, motto, vision and principles," Coach Kenny said. "You can have a great mindset, but if you don't have a mission, motto, vision and principles to guide your life, you have no foundation to build off of and you are not going to go anywhere.

"With no MVP Process, you will get distracted by the noise, the glitz and the glamour, just like you are right now, Matthew Simonds.

"Your mission, motto, vision and principles – your MVP Process – make up your championship culture. Your culture drives your decisions, it drives your behaviors, and it sets your standards. You must have an MVP Process and a championship culture for yourself, your family and your business. If you don't, you will crumble."

Coach Kenny was right. I had no mission, no motto, no vision and no principles. I was on the treadmill of life. Just running through the motions, running away or towards something – which one I wasn't sure. I just knew I was running and it was not in the direction I wanted to go; I just didn't know how to turn around.

"You know, Coach Kenny," I said. "When I played high school football, Coach Allen set up an MVP Process for us as a team. I never thought about doing that for myself or with my family."

"Do you remember what your MVP Process was on your high school football team?" Coach Kenny asked.

It was amazing, but I could clearly remember Coach Allen's MVP Process. It was 20 years ago and I can recall it as clear as day. Coach Allen used to model it, teach it and demand that we live it every day.

"I can. He used to say that our Mission was to be men who lived our principles on and off the field. That our Motto was Team First, Team Last. That our Vision was to win the league, district and state championship every year, and that our core Principles were to have disciplined daily habits and actions, to make a selfless commitment to others, to have a relentless positive energy, to have a progressive growth mindset, to be committed to excellence in all things all the time and to live with integrity and always do what was right."

As I spoke about the mission, motto, vision and principles Coach Allen shared with us during my high school football experience, I started getting emotional and the hair started sticking up on my body. I had been a part of a lot of teams in my life, both in athletics and in business, but none were as close as my high school football team. Some of my teammates were the best men in my wedding, the godfathers of my children and some of my closest friends, still 20 years later.

"Coach Allen used to tell us that the difference between a boy and a man was that a boy made decisions out of preference and a man made decisions out of principle," I said. "He challenged us every day to be men of principle and to live out the core principles of our program. I think as I get older, I realize more and more that he was teaching us not only how to win football games, but also how to win in life."

"Matthew Simonds, there is a tremendous crossover from what makes athletes and teams successful on the field to what makes people successful in life. The skills I learned in being an Olympic athlete have given me everything I have achieved outside of athletics," Coach Kenny said. "Have you ever thought about setting a mission, motto, vision and principles for yourself and your family?"

I was embarrassed. I had never even thought of doing this. I knew that 50%+ of marriages ended in divorce, and I bet almost all of the 50%+ did not have a mission, motto, vision and principles that served as the foundation of their marriage.

"Your mission is the bigger vision for your life; think about this as your eulogy. Your motto is your one-quarter to one-year mindset and focus. Your vision is what you want to accomplish based on long-term results. Think about your vision as more of your resume. Your principles are the core principles or core values and map that you follow on a daily basis to help achieve your vision."

I was finally starting to see how the MVP process came together and I needed one... yesterday.

CHAPTER 11

Pillar #3
Time Is Ticking

"Do you know what the only factor that every Olympic athlete, every corporate executive and every person in this airport right now has in common?" Coach Kenny asked.

"That we are all winners and learners?" I said.

"Very good." Coach Kenny said. "I see you workin,' – but no. That's not what I meant."

"I have no idea." I said with a smile.

"Time. Time is the ONLY factor that is the same for everyone on the planet. Time is the ONLY factor that is the same for every Olympic athlete, every corporate executive that wants the big contract, and for every high school football player and coach that wants to win on Friday night," Coach Kenny said.

"We are all given 86,400 seconds in a day and 168 hours in a week. No more. No less. How we choose to spend or invest that time will dictate almost everything in our lives.

"When I was training for the Olympics, I had a coach say to me one time: *Kenny, if you had a bank account that credited you with $86,400 every* *day and you were not allowed to take any money with you to the next day, and no matter how much you spent or how much you kept the next day you had $86,400 in your account, what you would you do?*

"I told him that I would either spend it all, give it all away or do something productive with it because the next day I would have $86,400 dollars again. What would you do with a bank account like that, Matthew Simonds?"

As I thought about it, the first thing that came to my mind was the #1 goal I had: to achieve financial security by paying off my house, eliminating any debt, having a strong financial safety net and living off interest.

"I think I would retire and spend as much time with Erin, Brina and Michael as I could," I said.

"Well, the first thing you must do is eliminate the word *spend* from your vocabulary and insert the word *invest* – that's part of the elite mindset and also part of knowing that your time is ticking. That's Pillar #3, Time Is Ticking. Matthew Simonds, you have that bank account with $86,400. It's called life, and you are given 86,400 seconds a day to invest or spend; it's up to you," Coach Kenny stated. "My next question is, do you know where your time is going? Are you in control of your time or is your time in control of you?"

As I finished my torrid pace of note taking on another napkin, I sat back and thought for a minute. Did I have any clue how much of my time every day was going towards my work vs. my family, my wealth vs. my health? I had no idea.

"Coach Kenny, I have always struggled with time management. I always try to get more done than I give myself time for and I end up getting stressed out and don't create the highest quality of work. I don't think any of my clients know the difference, but I do."

"If you know that you are not giving your very best, your clients do as well," Coach Kenny said. "If you are going to sign your name to something, it better be your very best work. Things that are built to last are not built fast, and we must keep our focus on doing work that is legendary and here forever vs. temporary and here today, gone tomorrow."

Things that are built to last are not built fast. Do work that is legendary, not temporary. I had heard these before. These were two of the motivational messages that Coach Allen had hung up in our locker room 20 years ago. He called them signs of success, SOS, and at the end of each season I would ask him for photocopies and hang them up in my room at home. He had a couple others that I remembered from one of his good friends and one of the top Lacrosse coaches in the country Morgan Randall: How you do anything is how you do everything. Excellence in small things is excellence in all things. Coach Randall was later featured in a book *Seeds of Success* by John Brubaker which had become one of my favorite reads.

Coach Kenny continued. "Time is a constant and is always ticking. We never know how much time we have left and we want to be sure we are taking as much control of our time as possible. You must create a system for how you map out your time, and I have an acronym for *system* I want to teach you."

S.Y.S.T.E.M.

Save

Yourself

Stress

Time

Effort, Energy

Motivation and Money

"I have a system where I sit down each Sunday night and map out my 168 hours for the week. I map out for each day when I am going to:

1. Go to sleep and wake up

2. When I am going to eat and prepare my food for the week

3. When I am going to do my recovery workouts like go to physical therapy, take an ice bath, do yoga, or get a massage

4. Lift weights, exercise, and do conditioning

5. Meditate

6. Do recreational sports like golf, tennis and walking

7. When I am going to read and do my professional development

8. Get ready, shower, dress, brush my teeth, do laundry, etc.

9. Transportation time such as driving or flying

10. Social time with my wife, friends, kids and grandkids

11. And my time for observing faith

"I map all of that out for the week on Sunday and then each night I look at my plan for the next day and see if that is still how I want to attack my day. Here, take a look."

Coach Kenny took out his cell phone and showed me how he mapped out his day in a program called Evernote on his phone. He said that he actually created it on his computer and then would maintain or update it on his phone as necessary. I was blown away at the detail he put into his plan for the week.

"Have you always mapped out your time like this?" I asked.

"I have now for about the last 60 years. We had a coach with the Olympics that stressed to us that being an Olympic champion was a lifestyle, not an event, and that winning a medal did not happen by accident, that it happened by intention. It happened by setting a course and a plan and then following it. This really struck a chord with me. I then met with him weekly for about a year until I learned to master his 168 plan technique. I used to do this in paper and pencil and now I do it on the computer and with my phone.

"It took me a while to change, but I had to stay up on the technology or I was going to get passed by," Coach Kenny said with pride. "I am a competitor and I was not going to let that happen. I won't be beat because of technology."

I was totally blown away by his attention to detail and the intentionality in which he planned his days. He had scheduled time for sending a text to his wife in the morning and for FTK-ing her at night. I had nothing like that on my schedule because I did not keep one written out; it was all in my head.

"Coach Kenny, this is awesome!" I said. "But I sort of feel like I am trying to drink from a fire hydrant right now. Where do I get started?"

"Matthew Simonds, remember, it's the start that stops most people. We will get you started. But before we get you started on your 12 Pillars of Peak Performance growth plan, we should finish going over the 12 Pillars themselves. You cool with that?"

I was totally cool with that.

"We will also need a refill on this beverage. All this talking is making me thirsty," Coach Kenny said.

As the waitress came and refilled our drinks, I plugged in my cell phone so that it wouldn't die during our talk. I wanted to capture all of this so I could listen to it again.

I was starting to get excited, really excited and a bit overwhelmed at the same time. I felt like I was back in a chalk talk with Coach Allen and my high school football teammates. I just couldn't write fast enough on these napkins. Thank God for cell phones and voice recorders, I thought. I was glad I could go back and listen to this again.

When the waitress was done topping off our drinks, Coach Kenny looked at her and said, "Thank you, Lynn."

"How did you know her name?" I asked in amazement.

"I asked her," he said. "When you know your server's name, you will get better service. It's a simple rule of life you should use. People don't care what you know till they know you care and the first way you show you care is to know someone's name."

With as often as I ate out, I was sure to write that one down.

"You know what the #1 motivator for all humans is, Matthew Simonds?"

"No, Coach Kenny, I don't," I said.

"Well, that's what you are going to learn in Pillars #4 & #5. But before we get into them, here is a cheers and a toast to my new friend, Matthew Simonds."

As we touched glasses and I took a sip, I felt like Coach Kenny's energy and passion for life had been transferred from his glass to mine, from his soul to my soul. I felt lit up and couldn't wait to hear what Pillars #4 & #5 were. I needed and wanted all the motivation I could get.

CHAPTER 12

Pillar #4
Know Your
Numbers

"Why do you think there are Olympic records?" Coach Kenny asked.

"So that we can experience the excitement of the chase and the exhilaration that comes from breaking a record?" I responded.

"It's much easier than that," Coach Kenny replied. "We keep records because measurement is motivation.

"In athletics, we keep all sorts of statistics to help measure how one performer matches up with another. In business, we focus on our essential metrics, and in education we make data-driven decisions," Coach Kenny said. "To accurately measure your progress and growth, you must know your numbers, and evaluating your numbers must become a routine part of your system."

The only number I ever measured was my bank account – how close I was to reaching my goal of financial security.

"You have to be careful, though, with your numbers, because you can do anything but you can't do everything," Coach Kenny said. "Starting with a few measurements done daily is better than trying to measure too many things at once. You also have to realize that not everything that matters can be measured, and not everything that can be measured matters. You must find the right numbers to measure."

"Do you have numbers that you measure on a routine basis as a part of your system?" I asked.

"I sure do." Kenny beamed. "I measure a lot of what goes into my 168 plan. I measure how much sleep I get; if I sent Brittany a nice message; what time I woke up; if Brittany and I FTK'd when I am on the road; if I exercised that day; what I ate that day in terms of macro nutrients, fat, carb and protein grams; if I did a form of meditation; how many phone calls to my friends I made; whether I called The Success Hotline; if I read *The Daily Dominator;* and how I felt my overall presence was with people that day."

Coach Kenny had a presence that I had never experienced. He had the perfect blend of intensity that you would get from an Olympic athlete and the sincerity and the love you would get from your grandfather. Unlike many of the people I worked with who seemed to care more about looking at their phones than they did you, Coach Kenny had not touched his phone since I met him other than when he was FTK-ing his wife. His presence was impressive.

"I simply keep a checklist with me by my bed and fill it out each morning when I wake up. I then go over it with my accountability partner, best friend, teammate and wife – the lovely and beautiful Brittany," Coach Kenny said as his face lit up with love.

"She is my rock, my everything. We have been together since we trained together for the Olympics. She has taught me more about life, liberty and the pursuit of excellence than anyone I know. She works back home in Southlake as a chiropractor, and she really takes measurements to another level. She measures how many patients come in each day, week, month, quarter and year. How many times and for what. She measures how many times she says *thank you*, how many times she makes a home-cooked meal. She loves her numbers and she is my #1."

As I sat there listening to him talk about his wife, I knew I needed to start measuring some sort of relationship deposit into my family. I needed to have a plan to rekindle the relationships I had neglected with Erin, Brina and Michael. I loved them and our twin French bulldogs Yotie and Cypress. We had named them after where Erin and I went on our first date, an Arizona Coyotes hockey game, and where I had proposed to her, at the Lone Cypress in Pebble Beach, California. I was determined to start measuring something – I just didn't know where to start.

"Coach Kenny, I know you said it was the start that stops most people," I said. "I want to get started with measuring something that will improve my relationships at home. I'm just at a bit of a loss; do you have any suggestions?"

"Well, I sure do," Kenny said with a smile. "Let's start with measuring how you are doing at Pillar #5."

-Measurement = Motivation

-You can do anything, you can't do everything

-It's the start that stops most people

-Things that are built to last are not built fast

SYSTEM
Save
Yourself
Stress
Time
Effort, Energy
Motivation & Money

Systems = Consistency

-If you are going to sign your name to something, it better be your best work

-Are you in control of your time or is your time in control of you?

-168 Hours in a week

-Move from spending to investing time

CHAPTER 13

Pillar #5
Sail the
Right Ships

"One of my running coaches used to say to me: *Kenny, running is an individual sport. Life is a team sport. You must learn to sail the right ships. You have to invest in relationships*. He would say that even though you compete in the decathlon as an individual, there are no individual sports, there are no individual athletes and no self-made men or women. We all need a team and we must invest into the relationships that matter most to us or, like muscles unattended to, they will become weak.

"That same coach had us measure the number of high fives we gave to our teammates at the track. At the time, I was young and thought this was stupid. Now, I give out high fives as much as I can because I have seen how much physical contact can enhance a relationship, and because high fives are free."

Just as he said that, Coach Kenny reached across the table and gave me a high five. Then he spun around and said, "Hey, Lynn, you are standing in a high five zone," and he gave her one as well.

When he sat back down and laughed, the smile on his face was a mile wide.

"Brittany and I started a high five zone in our house when our kids were little, and every time we walked by them in that space we would high five."

"Kind of like mistletoe during the holidays," I said.

"Just like mistletoe. Brittany and I actually have a piece of mistletoe hanging up in our bedroom year round. It is a constant reminder for us of the importance of physical contact. We also still use the high five zone in our house, even now when it's just the two of us. When the grandkids come over, they will stand in the high five zone for hours, counting how many they can get. It's a lot of fun."

As I thought more about it, Coach Allen used to encourage us to make contact with our teammates when coming on and off the field. I never knew why, but after hearing Coach Kenny talk, it all started to make sense.

"There was a study done at a school in California. They kept track of the number of times teammates in the NBA made physical contact with each other during a game," Coach Kenny said. "What they found was that the more a team touched, the more they won. I have shared that article with all of the coaches and athletes I work with. The ones that embrace contacts with each other and make it a part of their routine win more games. It's such a simple concept and so powerful. Usually it's the simple things that win. Especially today when as a society we are very sensitive to human touch and spend almost all of our waking hours touching a screen with our fingers."

The more I thought about it, the more excited I got about combining pillars #4 & #5. I was going to measure the amount of times I embraced my kids; the amount of times I slept in the same bed as Erin (which meant I was either home or she was traveling with me), which had significantly decreased over the years; and how many times I walked the dogs, either by myself to take that off Erin's plate or with either Brina or Michael so that I could get more quality time with them 1-1.

I was finally feeling as if I had a plan, or the start of one, that I could implement. The only issue was, I needed to be home to do it.

"You know, Matthew Simonds, people think there is a thing called balance in life. That we have a balance between work and life. I have never been great at that. There is one thing that I have been great at, and being great at this one thing probably helped me more as an athlete than anything else. It is the key to my marriage and is a huge part of what I teach to the coaches and athletes I work with," Coach Kenny said. "Do know what that one thing is?"

As Coach Kenny pointed his finger at me with a focus and intensity that made me feel like I was back in a football locker room getting ready to run out onto the field, I shook my head with an emphatic *yes*.

He looked me even deeper in the eye and said...

CHAPTER 14

Pillar #6 Present- Moment Focus

"Your focus determines your future. Your presence is the greatest gift you can give anything or anyone," Coach Kenny said. "Yesterday is history; tomorrow, that's a mystery; today is a gift – that's why we call it the present. Matthew Simonds, you must learn to be more present, to be where your feet are, so that you can experience each moment at the highest level."

Erin had always given me a hard time about hearing what she was saying but not listening to her, or for being there but not being present. I was starting to understand what she meant.

"Focus is the key that unlocks all doors. You can do anything with the right focus," Coach Kenny said. My grandson is a football player for the Carroll Dragons High School football team, which I think is one of the best, if not the best, high school football programs in the nation. Just the other day he was complaining about how bad the officials were in the last game and about how he felt like he was not getting a fair shot at the position he wanted to play, was not going to get a varsity letter or get to play at SMU, his dream school etc., etc. I wasn't having any of it.

"I told him, *Reno, you need to make a choice. You are either going to get bitter, or you are going to get better. That's up to you to decide.*"

Coach Kenny fired up from his seat and stepped to the side of the table.

"I told him that his problem was that he had one foot in the past, one foot in the future, and that he was crapping all over this present moment," Coach Kenny said as he got down into a squat like a person going to the bathroom in the woods. "You are beating yourself, son. You don't have to win a game or win a job; you just have to win a play today, that's all. Go do that! He got the point."

I started laughing, harder than I had laughed in a long time as Coach Kenny, still squatting, said again, "He was crapping all over the greatest gift there is, the gift of this present moment."

Coach Kenny then stood up and reached into his backpack and took out a magnifying glass. I had not seen one of those in years.

"To further make my point about the importance of a present-moment focus," Coach Kenny said, "I took him out to the backyard where in Southlake, Texas, it was still a cool 95 degrees in fall. I took a magnifying glass and handed it to him. I said 'Son, take the glass and move it around so that the sun goes through the glass and makes a little rainbow-colored circle on the ground. Then move that circle around and around on the grass and watch what happens.'

"Obviously, nothing happened," Coach Kenny said. "Then I had him get that rainbow-colored dot to stay on one piece of grass for a good minute. You know what happened? The grass started to burn. Smoke rose up and the grass caught on fire.

"That's exactly how your focus works. That's the gift of the present. For Reno, that was playing football one play at a time and living in the moment. Enjoying where he was at and what he was doing, not focusing so much on where he wanted to go and what he wanted to become that he missed this precious, present moment.

"For you Matthew Simonds, that is showing up with a presence and a focus that you have never brought before. It's a 100% commitment to the moment, to the people you are with, to your family, to your customers, to totally being where your feet are. There is no greater gift than your presence."

I couldn't agree more. In the rare chance I got to go see Michael play football, I spent more time on my phone setting up my fantasy football team than I did watching him play. I spent more time in my car listening to sports talk radio about the NFL than I did listening to audio books or podcasts that would help me learn to become more. I was learning from Coach Kenny that if I wanted more, I must become more, and that you didn't have to be sick to get better.

As Coach Kenny sat back down in his chair, he took a sip of his drink and asked, "You know why it's so hard to be present?"

"Because of this?" I said pointing to my cell phone. "Because we are on call 24/7?"

"No. A cell phone is a tool that can actually help you to be more present if you use it right. It puts the world at your fingertips. That's helpful," Coach Kenny said. "The reason why it's so hard to be present is because we focus on the wrong things and we attract more of what we focus on.

Our focus determines our future. Unfortunately, most people make the critical mistake that prevents them from being able to live in the present moment and that critical mistake is crushed with Pillar #7."

-There is no greater gift than your presence

-You don't have to be sick to get better

-Be where your feet are

-86,400 seconds in a day

-Yesterday is history, tomorrow is a mystery, today is a gift - that's why we call it the present

-Your focus determines your future

-Decisions determine destiny

CHAPTER 15

Pillar #7
Process over
Outcome

"Matthew Simonds, I am glad you like football. It's my favorite sport to watch," Coach Kenny said. "One of my clients is a big-time college football coach in the great state of Alabama and his whole program is based on Pillar #7. His whole program is based on putting the process over the result."

Process over result? I didn't understand. In college football, just as in my line of work as a business consultant, you were measured on one thing, results: wins and losses in football and bottom-line profits in business.

"What do you mean, Coach Kenny?" I asked. "Isn't it all about the win?"

Coach Kenny responded, "In the circles I run in, WIN stands for What's Important Now, and what's always most important is focusing on what you can control and letting go of what you can't – that's the process. That's the formula for success. That's also the mistake that most people make in performance – they focus on what they can't control more often than what they can and they beat themselves.

"This coach uses three critical mindset building statements, that we came up with together, with his team on a daily basis to reinforce the process, and I want to share these with you. So, please grab another napkin and write down Pillar #7 on top."

I reached for another napkin and was glad that I had been recording this entire conversation. I was going to listen to this again to make sure I was picking up all of what Coach Kenny was putting down. I was also going to buy a notebook and transfer all my napkins to paper. If I was prepared, I would have had one with me. Another sign I needed to raise my commitment in all areas of life.

"Are you ready?" Coach Kenny asked.

"Ready to roll," I said.

"Ok, here are three keys to the process from one of the best coaches in the world," Coach Kenny said.

1. "You must be in control of yourself before you can control your performance.

2. "You have very little control of what goes on around you, but total control of how you choose to respond to it.

3. "Your goal must be in your control.

"Matthew Simonds, in my 50+ years as a sport psychology consultant and in my work with coaches and athletes of all ages, I can tell you this: The #1 pitfall that they all fall into is focusing on what they can't control more than what they can," Coach Kenny stated. "When you, or anyone for that matter, is focusing on what you can't control, you are beating yourself; you are playing with one hand tied behind your back. Let's get super clear here. I want you to make a list on your napkin of all the things you can't control, that if you keep focusing on will make you beat yourself. Then I want you to make a list of what you can control on a separate napkin. While you do that, I am going to the bathroom."

Coach Kenny excused himself from the table and I started writing. As I started to write my list of things I couldn't control, I was blown away by how long it was. As I wrote my list of what I could control, I was shocked at how short it was. I was really only in control of myself, my attitude and actions, my preparation and performance, my effort and energy.

"Matthew Simonds, here's what I want you to do," I heard Coach Kenny say over my shoulder as he returned from the bathroom. "Take that list of what you can't control, take it to the bathroom with you and flush it down the toilet. That's exactly what you need to do with what you can't control. You need to flush it!"

I liked where he was going. I needed to go to the bathroom, and I wanted to let go of all the stuff I couldn't control and focus on what I could. There was just one problem. I had put Erin, Brina, Michael, Yotie, and Cypress on the list of non-controllables and was not about to flush them down the toilet.

"Coach Kenny, where do you put your family? You can't really control them, can you? I don't want to flush them down the toilet."

"They are in your area of influence," he said. "There are aspects of life that you can control, areas that you can't control and areas that you can influence. Right now we want to get you focused on what you can control and to let go of what you can't. You are right in that you can't control what your wife, kids and dogs do – but you can control how much of yourself that you invest into them, and you can control your response to what they do and what they say. If you maximize what you can control you should be able to have maximum impact and influence with them. Another football coach I work with gave his players a rubber wrist band like this as a constant reminder."

Coach Kenny rolled up his sleeve and showed me a gray silicone band around his wrist that had E+R=O written on it in red.

"That stands for Event + Response = Outcome. We are not in control of the events that happen to us and we don't control the outcome, but we always control the response we take in any situation, and that will influence the outcome," Coach Kenny said. "We must focus on our response. Viktor Frankl wrote about choosing your response to adversity in *Man's Search For Meaning*, Marcus Luttrell wrote about this in *The Lone Survivor*, and Louis Zamperini demonstrated this through his story *Unbroken*.

"Focusing on what you can control and on the process gives you the best chance for success and for getting the outcome you want," Coach Kenny stated. "The crazy thing is, you get less outcome when you focus on outcome. You get more outcome when you focus on process."

I thought I knew what coaches he was referring to, but I wasn't going to ask because I did not want him to break his confidentiality. I had read all three of those books but read them for entertainment, not for education. I should have read them as a man on a mission to find something of value that I could apply to my life. I had missed those critical points.

Controlling what you can control. Focusing not on the events or the outcome, but on your response to those events. I loved it, and I wanted to live it. As I got up from the table to go to the restroom to flush the napkin where I had written down all of the things I could not control, I started to think about what I was going to do next.

I was still in Detroit. It was still Wednesday and I still had no plan for how I was getting home. It looked like my next flight wasn't until Saturday. I was loving my time with Coach Kenny, but I wanted to get home now more than ever. I thought hard about getting a rental car and driving the 17.5 hours back to Southlake, TX. If I had to sleep in the car, I could, that wouldn't be the first time. I was determined to get home and make this right. I knew I could either find a way or find an excuse. But first, I was going to find out what Pillar #8 was all about.

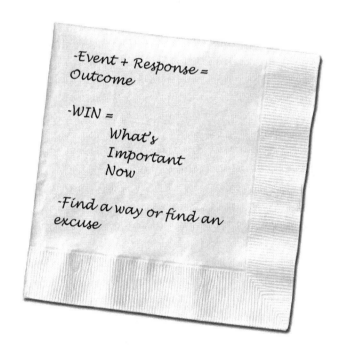

-Event + Response = Outcome

-WIN =
  What's
  Important
  Now

-Find a way or find an excuse

-Control what you can control

-You get less outcome when you focus on outcome; you get more outcome when you focus on process

-We are not in control of the events that happen to us but we always control the response

CHAPTER 16

Pillar #8
Attitude
Determines
Altitude

As I walked back from the bathroom to the table in Fuddruckers where Coach Kenny was sitting, I noticed that he was on the phone. I stopped, took out my phone and recorded a short selfie video message for Erin and the kids.

"Hey, loves of my life. Hope you are safe and cozy. Dad's stuck in Detroit and is working to find a way home to see you so that we can have turkey and watch the Cowboys tomorrow and celebrate Mom's big day on Friday. Michael, be nice to your sister and Brina, be nice to your mother. Erin, I love you, babe. Hold the fort down as you always do when I am gone. Give Yotie a belly scratch for me and run the dent in Cypress's forehead. I will let you all know when I know more. I love you."

As I hit *send* on that message to Erin, I saw Coach Kenny waving me over to the table. I was determined to send them a message every day that I was gone to help invest in our relationship, and I was going to measure it.

When I sat down, I overheard Coach Kenny on the phone.

"Six months – well, that's better than a year, brother. Stay positive and remember that your attitude determines your altitude and that the more positive you are, the faster the body heals. Be strong. Attack your rehab and never feel sorry for yourself. Knees heal. Compared to what it could have been, you are lucky. Remember that keeping a compared to what mindset will help keep you from feeling sorry for yourself. Now dominate rehab, one day at a time."

As he hung up, he took a deep breath and said to me, "Injuries suck. Especially the freak ones."

"If you don't mind me asking, what happened?" I wanted to know.

"One of my clients is a world champion mixed martial artist and had a big title fight coming up next month. He was jumping on a trampoline with his kids when the tramp springs broke and he fell to the ground. Luckily, he was the only one on that part of the tramp and his kids are fine, but he tore his ACL and is now out for at least 6 months," Coach Kenny said. "I told him to stay strong, to stay positive – that negativity only slows down recovery and that if he started to feel sorry for himself to simply think of a *compared to what* scenario to help get his mind right.

"Compared to what could have happened if it was his kids that fell through the tramp and not him," Coach Kenny said. "It could have been a whole lot worse. He will be fine. I feel for him, yet at the same time, everyone else is going to feel sorry for him, and he can't let himself feel sorry for him. Feeling sorry for yourself is a worthless emotion. He needs to remember that his attitude determines his altitude and that the attitude he takes is always a decision he makes."

As I grabbed for another napkin to write down "the attitude you take is a decision you make," I was reminded of something that Coach Allen used to teach us in football that I understood more the older I got.

He used to tell us that the more energy we gave the more energy we would get. That energy was a life cycle and if your energy was negative, you would get more negative energy, and if your energy was positive, you would get more positive energy. He would say that energy attracts and energy is contagious; he would then ask if our energy was worth catching or avoiding.

Coach Kenny sure fit this mold and at close to 80 years old, I was starting to think he might be the most energetic person I had ever met.

"How do you stay so positive?" I asked him.

"You know, I wasn't always the most positive guy, especially when I was younger," Coach Kenny said. "I am a learned optimist. I have learned the power of positive thinking and I have learned to have an attitude of gratitude.

"One of my clients, a professional baseball player, sent me a video of a guy he had worked with in the mental game of baseball when he was playing in college at TCU. The video was of this coach, whose name escapes me, talking about The GHP Principle and was a part of a video series called *The Monday Message*. I am sure you can find it online by doing a search for *The Monday Message*, GHP Principle," Coach Kenny said.

"The GHP Principle is that if you express more gratitude, you will experience more happiness and that will lead to a better performance. The principle states that as gratitude goes up, so does your happiness and so does your performance,"

Coach Kenny explained. "I started an attitude of gratitude journal on my phone and every day I simply write down one thing I'm grateful for. This has been like lifting weights for my mindset happiness and for my positivity. Matthew Simonds, you have got to start keeping a gratitude journal."

I was thinking the same thing after hearing Coach Kenny speak with such enthusiasm about his gratitude journal.

"The other big way I have become more positive is by implementing Pillar #9 on a daily basis," Coach Kenny said.

I couldn't wait to hear what Pillar #9 was all about. I needed more positivity in my life.

-Keep a compared to what mentality

-The attitude you take is a decision you make

-The more positive you are, the faster the body heals

-Energy is contagious, is yours worth catching or avoiding?

-The more energy you give, the more energy you have, it's a cycle

CHAPTER 17

Pillar #9
Everything
Happens Twice

An Attitude of Gratitude Journal. I was going to start that one up immediately. I also wanted to know the second strategy Coach Kenny used to be more positive. I felt like I had been in a rut for a while and meeting Coach Kenny was helping me to get out of that rut.   I wanted more positivity and optimism in my life and was willing to pretty much try anything at this point.

"The second strategy I use on a daily basis to help me be more positive, confident and prepared for a great day is mental imagery," Coach Kenny said. "I will sit and close my eyes, and in my mind's eye I will imagine myself performing and my day unfolding exactly like I want it to. It's like watching a highlight video of my day before I live it. The Blue Angels, the Navy's best pilots that fly those amazing air shows, use imagery; and all the athletes I work with have a custom mental imagery audio that they listen to each day to help keep their minds right and see themselves performing how they want to perform.   We record that on their phones using that same app that you are using to record our talk here, that voice memos app."

"You mean recording this life-changing coaching session?" I said. "Coach Kenny, I have a question for you. Is mental imagery the same thing as visualization? We had a performance coach come in and train us in how to take our clients through visualization, and I have never been comfortable enough to do it on my own with them. Maybe that's because I don't use visualization myself?"

"It's hard to teach others what we don't do ourselves. I actually think that's the definition of hypocrite. Asking others to do what you are not doing.

"Yes, mental imagery and visualization are the same thing. They are both different than just thinking about your job or performance. A lot of us daydream, and to a certain degree that can be productive. Daydreaming is when you quickly see yourself doing what you want to do or acting how you want to act, and it happens in a matter of seconds and is unscripted and unplanned.

"Mental imagery, on the other hand, is when you sit or lie down for three to thirty minutes and go through an exact routine for getting relaxed, affirming how you want to act or think, and then you recall your previous best performances and rehearse for your next performance. Mental imagery is much more structured than daydreaming.

"The reason why imagery is effective is that the human brain cannot tell the difference between what you physically experience and what you vividly imagine. The brain processes them both with the same psychoneuromuscular pathways, which in English means you have a physiological or a body response to a psychological or mental stimulus.

"It's just like when you are at a scary movie and a guy jumps out of a closet with an axe and you jump out of your seat," Coach Kenny said. "There is no danger to you, but your brain cannot tell the difference. Thus, you have a physiological/body response.

"The problem is that most people never tap into the power of structured mental imagery, and in the world of sport psychology we believe that you never outperform your self-image and that everything happens twice: first in your mind, then in reality. If you want to strengthen your self-image, mental imagery is as good of a way to do that as anything else."

I had not done any mental imagery or visualization since high school when Coach Allen would talk us through how we were going to play before we took the field. I used to love those sessions. I could actually feel myself throwing a touchdown, I could hear the crowd, I could smell the hot dogs that they grilled in the concession stand right behind our team bench. I could smell the amazing soups that they brought in from the world-famous 4-Acers Restaurant in our town and sold in small plastic helmets. Now I understood why he did that and why my boss brought in someone to teach us how to take my clients through mental imagery. I wondered why I had not used mental imagery in my own life, with my clients or with my kids? I needed to get back to doing this.

"Coach Kenny, I feel like you are giving me the keys to the kingdom of my future, yet I feel like there is so much for me to do to get caught up that I don't know where to start. How do I get it all done?" I asked.

"Well, Matthew Simonds, you know what to do – you just are not doing what you know. Rome was not built in a day, and you will not get yourself out of the present situation you got yourself into

123
@BrianCainPeak

over the last few years in a day either. It will take some time," Coach Kenny said. "The 12 Pillars of Peak Performance is a lifestyle, not a magic bullet. Remember, what's built to last is not built fast and the number one way to implement all of the pillars into your life on a consistent basis is by understanding Pillar #10..."

-You never out-perform your self image

-The best way to enhance your self-image is with imagery and visualization

- Everything happens twice, first in your mind, then in reality

-Mental Imagery and visualization are the same thing

-The reason why imagery is effective is that the human brain cannot tell the difference between what you physically experience and what you vividly imagine

CHAPTER 18

Pillar #10
Routines &
Habits of
Excellence

"Pillar #10 is just as important as any other pillar," Coach Kenny said. "The pillars are sequential and in the order that they are in because we want to have a rock-solid foundation and build off of each of the previous pillars. We want to have the right foundation to build our routines and habits of excellence on because we become what we do on a daily basis. First we make our habits and then our habits make us. Pillar #10 is about creating routines and habits of excellence."

Coach Kenny then reached for his iPhone and slid it across the table.

"Matthew Simonds. Do you like to fish?" he asked.

"I LOVE fishing. I hardly ever get to go," I replied as two of my favorite pictures I had hung up in my office came to mind. The first was a picture of Erin and me fly-fishing in Alaska, and the second was her holding a largemouth bass the size of her quad (and she was a hockey player) that she had caught with one of the best fishing guides in Texas, Heath Autrey. It was the biggest bass I had ever seen and she caught it... with a lot of help from Heath.

"Well, I love fishing as well," Coach Kenny said. "And I love teaching a man to fish, more than catching him a fish.

"I want you to open up that app right there," he said, as he pointed to a green square with an elephant's head on it. "It's called Evernote. I live in that app. It's where I capture all of my thoughts so that I never lose them and so that I don't have to remember anything and can let the creative juices flow. It keeps me organized."

As I clicked on the Evernote App, up popped what looked like a library of three-ring binders. There was one for each of the 12 pillars, and there was one for what looked like each of Coach Kenny's clients.

"Click on that binder called Pillar #10," Coach Kenny suggested. "Then scroll down to the page that says Poems and Quotes."

As I scrolled though what looked like Coach Kenny's library of research and life's work, I found the binder called Pillar #10 and the note that said Poems and Quotes.

"Is this it?" I asked as I showed him the screen.

"That's the one. Go ahead and read that," Coach Kenny said.

I am your constant companion.

I am your greatest helper or your heaviest burden.

I will push you onward or drag you down to failure.

I am completely at your command.

Half the things you do,
you might just as well turn over to me,
and I will be able to do them quickly and correctly.

I am easily managed;
you must merely be firm with me.

Show me exactly how you want something done,
and after a few lessons I will do it automatically.

I am the servant of all great men.

And, alas, of all failures as well.

Those who are great, I have made great.

Those who are failures, I have made failures.

*I am not a machine, though I work
with all the precision of a machine.*

Plus, the intelligence of a man.

*You may run me for profit, or run me for ruin;
it makes no difference to me.*

*Take me, train me, be firm with me
and I will put the world at your feet.*

Be easy with me, and I will destroy you.

Who am I?

I am a HABIT!

Author Unknown

"Wow! I need better habits," I said.

"We all do," Coach Kenny replied. "First we make our habits and then our habits make us. I used to think that we rose to the occasion and could flip a switch when the lights came on. Then I had a coach at one of our Olympic training camps say to me that as athletes, we don't rise to the occasion – we sink to our levels of training and habits. I thought that was so profound. That mindset about the importance of sinking to our levels of training and habits has stuck with me for over 50 years. Even as I say it today, I can clearly see the image of him saying that to us at the track in Oregon where we were training at the time.

"The key to having great habits is being able to have routines, and the key to having great routines is to have habits. My wife tells me that I am a machine of routine. She gets on me for setting an alarm clock each night because I have woke up before my alarm clock for the last 50 years. I don't know if it even works, but my routine clock sure does."

I could not remember the last time I woke up before my alarm clock. It might have been when

Brina used to scream in her crib and Erin would go get her and the dogs would start barking and then my mind would start racing and I would get up, make a pot of bulletproof coffee and start checking e-mail. The only routine I had in my life was swiping my phone screen to snooze and trying to sleep as long as possible, putting off what had to be done that day.

"Matthew Simonds, the secrets of success are hidden in the routines of your daily life," Coach Kenny stated. "The golfers I work with know all about routine. The kickers I work with in the NFL know all about routine. It's one of life's great secrets that you become what you do on a daily basis. But it's no longer a secret for you, Matthew Simonds, because I just told you."

"You are so right, Coach Kenny." I chuckled at his joke about one of life's great secrets no longer being a secret. "I feel like you are telling me all of life's great secrets. Meeting you has been amazing."

"Thank you for you kind words, Matthew Simonds," Coach Kenny said. "But, let me ask you this. How much of what we have talked about have you ever heard before?"

As I sat back and thought about it... I had heard almost all of what Coach Kenny was saying at various points in my life; I had just never heard it all put into such an easy and organized system as the 12 Pillars of Peak Performance.

"Almost all of it," I answered.

"You are like most people," Coach Kenny said. "And we call that average. I hate the word average. It means you are the best of the worst and the worst of the best. It's a terrible place to live. You know what to do; you just don't do what you know because you don't have a routine and you don't have an accountability partner. Once we get you a routine, you will start living the life you want to live. I will be your accountability partner to help you along the way. But, there's also one more thing you don't have. It's pillar #11."

-We become what we do on a daily basis

-First we make our habits and then our habits make us

-Don't catch a man a fish, teach him how to fish

-We don't rise to the occasion, we sink to the levels of our training and habits

-The secrets of success are hidden in the routines of your daily lives

-Don't be average, it means you are the best of the worst and the worst of the best and is a terrible place to live

Pillar #11
Recognize Your
Signal Lights

"What you don't have, Matthew Simonds, is exactly what the best coaches and athletes I work with have more than anyone else," Coach Kenny said. "It's trainable. It's also the most difficult of all the 12 Pillars to develop. You know what it is?"

I had no idea, and I could not wait to find out.

"It's what I call ATW. Awareness To Win. Awareness is knowing what's going on around you and inside of you at all times. It's being able to respond to your response. It's being able to check in on your mental and emotional state and then being able to adjust that mental and emotional state accordingly to keep yourself in the best state for a peak performance in that moment."

I was a little lost. I wasn't totally following what he was saying. I didn't want to show Coach Kenny that I couldn't totally understand what he was talking about because I didn't want him to think I wasn't with him. Then I remembered what Burt Watson, a friend and a legend in the mixed martial arts world, said once: *The only dumb question is the one you don't ask.*

"Coach Kenny, I am not sure I totally understand ATW and awareness to win." I said. "Can you explain it more? I want to know what it is so that I can live all of the 12 Pillars of Peak Performance."

"Matthew Simonds, think about awareness as a signal light when you are driving a car. When you get to the signal light, if it's green, it tells you to go; if it's red, it tells you to stop. If it's yellow, it tells you to slow down or speed up," Coach Kenny said with a chuckle. "Awareness is just like driving that car. In life, when you are in a positive state, feel good, are getting results and like the way things are rolling for you, we call that a green light state.

"When you are in a negative state and things are moving really fast or slow for you, you don't feel good, and you are not getting the results you want, we call that a red light state. Most of the time in life we operate in a yellow light state. We are in neutral and we either move ourselves towards a positive, green light state or a negative, red light state based on what we choose to focus on, how we choose to speak to ourselves and how we choose to carry ourselves physically.

"Matthew Simonds, please stand up, please stand up. Would the real Matthew Simonds please stand up, please stand up." Coach Kenny said this in rhythm to the song *Slim Shady* by Eminem.

"You listen to Eminem?" I asked while laughing.

"Look, when you work the athletes like I do, you have to read what they read, watch what they watch and listen to what they listen to or you'll become extinct," Coach Kenny said. "Eminem gets me fired up; I will listen to his stuff when I run, that is, when I am not listening to an audio book, which is what I do 90% of the time. Audio books as I run – yes sir, that's another key part of my routine."

I laughed standing there. Here I was, out of shape, in my mid 30's, finding every excuse in the world to not run or do yoga, which Erin and the kids did together almost every day, and this 80-year-old savage was running every day, listening to audio books and Eminem, keeping a journal and living life at the highest level.

"Matthew Simonds. Stand big and tall and pull your shoulders back. Now close your eyes and think of a time in your life when you were at your best," Coach Kenny said with a strong and positive tone.

I thought of the last vacation Erin and I had taken. We were on a cruise with friends to the Bahamas. This was before the kids were born. We were out on the dance floor having a great time dancing together to a song by DJ Gulian called *Back That Azz Up*. It was one of the most fun times of my life and probably the last time I had danced full out without a care in the world of what other people were thinking or saying. As I put myself back on that boat and on that dance floor, I could feel myself getting bigger, smiling wider and getting into a green light state.

"That's it," Coach Kenny said. "That's the green light state. I can see it in you. Can you feel it?"

I nodded my head and opened my eyes.

"Good. Now I want you to close your eyes again and think of a time when you were at your worst, a time when you were in a red light state," Coach Kenny said with a depressed tone of voice.

This was much easier for me. It had been a long time ago that I was in a true green light state. All

I had to do to bring back a red light state was remember how my phone call with Erin, just an hour or so earlier, made me feel after she told me how disappointed she and the kids were that it looked like I was not going to be home for Thanksgiving or her birthday. I immediately felt my shoulders slump and my head go down from where it was when I was in the green light state. I felt much smaller.

"Do you feel that difference?" Coach Kenny asked.

"Yes, I feel smaller and heavier than I did in the green light state." I said. "I feel like this is how I live most of the time."

"Not any more, you don't," Coach Kenny responded as he sat up from the table, put his two hands on my shoulders and looked me straight in the eye.

"You are in charge of your states at all times. You can get back to this green light state anytime you want. Your states never leave you. They are always inside of you. You have the responsibility to learn how to get yourself into a green light state all the time. Go green for yourself, for Erin, for Brina, for Michael, for the people you serve on your mission as a business consultant. People are counting on you to be in green lights, Matthew Simonds. Your family needs you to be at your best. The people you serve need you to be at your best. The world needs you to be at your best, Matthew Simonds!"

I don't know why, but tears started pouring our of my eyes and I become over come with emotion as I stood there in Fuddruckers at the Detroit airport with Coach Kenny having his hands on my shoulders. I felt a flood of emotion that I had not felt in years. I had learned to bury my emotions and just put my head down and keep grinding. It was like all those years of keeping those emotions inside were coming out of me.

"I just don't know how to get out of the red light state. I feel like such a loser," I said fighting through the tears and the emotion.

"Matthew Simonds, how many pillars have we covered?" Coach Kenny asked.

"Eleven. We have covered 11," I said.

"Well, I have good news for you, son." Coach Kenny gently squeezed my shoulders. "Pillar #12 is going to give you the exact steps to be able to go from red to green that fast." He snapped his fingers. "The world needs you to be a machine of green."

I was ready to get out of this red light state and learn how to tap into the green light state as often as possible.

-Awareness is knowing what's going on around you and inside of you

-You must respond to your response

-The only dumb question is the one that you don't ask

-People like people who are like them

-Green = Positive
-Yellow = Neutral
-Red = Negative

CHAPTER 20

Pillar #12
Release &
Refocus

I finally understood the difference between a red light and green light state. I wanted to learn how to get into a green light state and stay there.

As Coach Kenny and I sat back down at our table, Lynn, the waitress, came over and gave us our check. I grabbed it first and Coach Kenny quickly put his hand on top of mine.

"I told you earlier that I was not taking any new clients and that I was buying this dinner," he said. "Do not deny the pleasure I will receive for buying you dinner, Matthew Simonds."

"Coach Kenny, please. Let me get this," I said.

"Your money is no good here," Coach Kenny replied. "One of my friends owns this Fuddruckers. I got this."

He took out a crisp $100 bill and wrote a message on it: *For the lovely Lynn. Thank you for your service. Keep smiling.* He then put the $100 bill under the check.

We got up and started walking out of the restaurant, but not before I could glimpse down at the bill and saw that it was for zero dollars.

"Coach Kenny, were those burgers and drinks for free?" I asked.

"No, they cost the owner of the restaurant what they cost financially to produce. They cost the chef the time to make them; Lynn the time to bring them to us; the farmer who grew the mushrooms, onion and peppers the time to grow them; the farmer who cut the grain the time to grow it; the baker that made the buns the time to bake it; and above all else, the cows who provided the milk for the cheese and the meat for the burger the time to produce the milk and their lives. There's a lot more that goes into making the world's greatest hamburger than we think," Coach Kenny said. "We take for granted the simple things like being able to get a hamburger that tastes that good as easily as walking up to the counter and ordering."

"That's a great point. I never thought of that. Pretty amazing all that goes into a hamburger and all that we take for granted," I said. "I noticed on the bill that there was a zero balance and you left a $100 bill."

"I gave Lynn my credit card when you went to the bathroom and told her to NOT let you pay for this," Coach Kenny said as we started walking out of the restaurant. "That $100 was for her service. She was great. And that note I left her. That's a part of my routine. If I can do anything to help make someone's day a little bit brighter, I do it. It takes no skill to be positive and to help brighten up someone's day and put them into a green light state."

As we started walking down the terminal, following signs towards the airport hotel, I wanted to know how to get out of a red light state and into a green light state as fast as possible.

I knew that Lynn would go green when she got her $100 tip, and Coach Kenny was in green from giving it to her. I still felt red from thinking about how far I had drifted off course since that great night on the cruise and how I was going to get home ASAP.

"You know, Matthew Simonds," Coach Kenny said, "the most challenging and rewarding part of the 12 Pillars of Peak Performance is recognizing your signal lights and having the awareness to win. Could you feel the difference when I had you stand up just a few minutes ago and go green and then go red?"

"I sure could – it was crazy," I said.

"I knew you could. I could see it in your entire being," Coach Kenny replied. "Now that you have an idea of what it means to recognize your signal lights, the next step is to master Pillar #12, to release and refocus. You have to be able to let go of the negative so that you can grow the positive. Let the negative go and let the positive grow."

"That makes sense, Coach Kenny," I said. "But how do you do it? I hear people say you have to be positive all the time, but that's easier said than done."

"The first step is to recognize that you are in a red light state. Once you do that, you go through a release ritual and 'flush it,'" Coach Kenny said, making a movement with his hand of flushing a toilet.

"Like when you had me go to the bathroom to flush away the napkin with all of the things I could not control on it?" I asked.

"That's exactly it. The physical act of flushing the toilet is a release. The physical act of doing something to associate with flushing it is exactly what a release is. It might be clapping your hands, crumpling up a piece of paper and throwing it away, making a fist or tightening a part of your body and then letting it go or stomping your feet, but do something to let it go and flush it."

"Brina is good at that. She stomps her feet all the time when she is in red lights," I said, laughing as I thought about my little girl stomping away in frustration.

"You know what, though? She is amazing. She will always come skipping back seconds later with another request and a huge smile on her face. She can go from red to green that fast," I said as I snapped my fingers.

"Sounds like she has a good release already," Coach Kenny said. "Most of us have a physical release that we do naturally, but because we don't have the awareness and an association that what we physically do is our release of that red light and negative energy, we are inconsistent with it.

"After we release, we have to refocus and one of the best ways to refocus is to talk to yourself, not listen to yourself. When we are in red lights, we listen to ourselves and we can get back to green lights by talking to ourselves."

I was a little confused. I did not know the difference between talking to and listening to myself.

"When you get into red lights, think of a little character dressed in red we call negative Nancy or negative Ned. This character tells you how you are no good, how you got cheated, how you should quit, that it's not worth it or not fair, etc. When you listen to that negative voice, you are listening to yourself.

"On the other shoulder is a character dressed in green that we call positive Paula or positive Paul. This character speaks to you with the voice of reason, talking to you about what's important now, about what you can do positively and constructively to improve your position in this moment, about what you can control," Coach Kenny said. "When you talk to yourself, it's this voice speaking. When you talk to yourself, you can use this voice to refocus you back to the moment.

"When you listen to yourself, you get stuck in the past or projected into the future, and in either place, you will drown in a sea of negativity. When you talk to yourself, you can do anything," Coach Kenny stated.

"So, when we listen to ourselves it's negative and when we talk to ourselves it's positive?" I asked for clarification.

"That's about right," Coach Kenny answered. "Look, everyone has their own ways of recognizing their signal lights, releasing and refocusing. The most simple way I can teach it is like this, and it has worked for mostly everyone who uses it.

"When you recognize red lights, have a physical release to flush your red lights and then talk yourself back into green lights using a trigger word or phrase like *right here, right now*."

Just as Coach Kenny had finished saying *right here right now*, we were in the lobby at the airport hotel.

-It takes no skill to be positive and to help brighten up someone's day

-Let go of the negative so that you can grow the positive

-The best way to refocus is to talk to yourself, not to listen to yourself.

CHAPTER 21

The Airport Hotel Lobby

"Well, Coach Kenny," I said. "Looks like this might be the end of the road?"

"Never the end of the road, Matthew Simonds, always a bend in the road," Coach Kenny said. "I told you I was not taking on any more clients... because I don't have any."

"What do you mean you don't have any clients?" I asked. "The guy that owned the Fuddruckers? The MMA world champion that fell through the trampoline you were on the phone with earlier – aren't those guys your clients?"

"I don't think of them as clients. I think of them as friends, family and teammates," Coach Kenny said. "I was an individual sport athlete and never had any close teammates when I was younger. I missed out on that experience, and as I evolved, I realized the power of friends, family and teammates. Team might be the most powerful word in the world. I see myself as a teammate and friend to the people in my life that most people call clients. I am not taking any more clients, but I would be honored to be your friend and teammate."

I loved that perspective. Treat your clients like friends, family and teammates. Team is the most powerful word in the world. Team and friends were genius. And team and friends were missing from my life.

"Coach Kenny, I don't only want you to be my friend and on my team. I need you to be my friend, mentor, coach and teammate. Tonight has been life changing. I am going to put the 12 Pillars of Peak Performance into use immediately," I said. "Boy, am I glad I sat next to you on the plane! What is one of the worst things that could happen to me today has turned out to be one of the best."

"That too, Matthew Simonds, is a principle of life," Coach Kenny responded. "Turn the worst things that happen to you into the best."

"This is one layover I will remember for the rest of my life. Please, let me get you a room here at this airport hotel," I said. "I have so many points from traveling that I can get us each a room for free."

Then I heard a voice from behind the desk...

159

CHAPTER 22

Sold Out

"Excuse me, sir. Sir."

I walked to the front desk and approached the woman who was speaking. She was the general manager of the hotel.

"I hate to say this, but we are all sold out tonight. We have no rooms available," she said.

"No rooms available!" I said in frustration and I threw my hands in the air. "You have to be kidding me. Can you call any of your other properties in the area and see if they have any rooms available?"

"I am so sorry, sir," the woman replied. "We have been turning people away all night and have called every hotel within an hour's drive, and they are all sold out as well. With tomorrow being Thanksgiving, and with the Detroit Lions undefeated this season playing at home against the Chicago Bears who are also undefeated coupled with the Detroit Marathon this weekend, it seems like everyone is in Detroit at the same time. I'm so sorry."

As I clapped my hands hard, and took a big deep breath to release, I turned around to see what Coach Kenny was going to do.

He was nowhere to be seen.

I had no idea where he went – he was just there a minute ago.

There I was.

Standing at the airport hotel counter in the Detroit airport.

Alone.

I didn't know what I was going to do.

All I knew was I needed to find a way to get home and start applying the 12 Pillars of Peak Performance before it was too late.

Want to know what Matthew Simonds does next?

Continue the journey by visiting BrianCain.com/EliteMindset

ABOUT THE AUTHOR

Brian M. Cain, MS, CMAA, is a #1 best-selling author, speaker, coach and expert in the fields of Mental Conditioning, Peak Performance, Organizational Leadership and Character Education.

He has worked with coaches, athletes, and teams at the Olympic level and in the National Football League (NFL), National Basketball Association (NBA), National Hockey League (NHL), Ultimate Fighting Championship (UFC), on the Professional Golf Tour (PGA) and in Major League Baseball (MLB).

Cain has spoken on stages all over the world and has delivered his system at clinics, corporate retreats, leadership summits, and conventions.

Highly sought after, Cain delivers his message with passion, in an engaging style that keeps his audiences energized, focused and empowered through the learning process.

As someone who lives what he teaches, Cain will inspire you and, more importantly, give you the tools necessary to get the most out of your career and life.

CONNECT WITH CAIN
ON SOCIAL MEDIA

 @BrianCainPeak

 /BrianCainPeak

 /BrianCainPeak

 /BrianCainPeak

 @BrianCainPeak

WHERE'S CAIN?

Find out when Brian will be in your area and inquire about having him come educate, energize, and empower you and your team or organization!

View Cain's Calendar at
BrianCain.com/Calendar

Contact Cain by visiting
BrianCain.com/Contact

MONDAY MESSAGE

Want to receive tips, techniques, strategies and stories to help you close the gap from where you are to where you want to be?

Get Cain's Monday Message delivered directly to your Inbox each week!

Join now at
BrianCain.com/Monday

"We review the Monday Message every week as part of our weekly routine and mindset management. It has served as a great resource for our staff and players and keeps Cain's system in the forefront of their minds."

Tony Reno
Head Football Coach
Yale University

PODCAST

Every Wednesday, Cain takes you inside the locker rooms, coaches' offices and meeting rooms of the best teams in the country. Learn how the best of the best use this program to maximize their potential in their life and competitive arena.

Subscribe on iTunes now at
BrianCain.com/Podcast

View Archives at
BrianCain.com/Blog

PRODUCTS

Brian Cain is a #1 best-selling author of more than 30 books and training programs that are being used by Champions around the world.

If you're looking for the best of the best when it comes to Mental Conditioning, Performance Psychology, Organizational Leadership, Team Building and Character Education, look no further. Cain's world-class product selection will help you maximize your potential and become a Master of the Mental Game.

View all of Cain's Products at
BrianCain.com/Products

THE
BRIAN CAIN

Want to master the 12 Pillars of Peak Performance in your life? Get your total immersion learning experience by attending Cain's next live 2-day event.

Reserve your spot now at
BrianCain.com/Experience

Go deep inside 1 of the 12 Pillars of Peak Performance by attending Cain's next live 1-day Bootcamp.

Reserve your spot now at
BrianCain.com/Bootcamp

INNER CIRCLE

Want to be the best? Surround yourself with like-minded individuals who are on the same mission as you by joining Cain's Inner Circle. As an Inner Circle member, you'll receive:

- Monthly Audio & Corresponding Newsletter
- Weekly Monday Message Worksheets
- Exclusive Access to Private Facebook Group
- Reserved Inner Circle Seating at Live Events
- and much more...

Join today by visiting
BrianCain.com/InnerCircle

"You become the average of the 5 people you surround yourself with most."

Brian Cain

KEYNOTE SPEAKING

Cain has spoken on stages all over the world and delivers *The 12 Pillars of Peak Performance* at retreats, clinics, leadership summits, and conventions. Cain will inform, inspire and give you the proven strategies and systems necessary to get the most out of your career and life.

Book Cain to speak at your next event!
BrianCain.com/Speaking

TEAM CONSULTING

Brian Cain is the coach that top university and high school athletic teams turn to for a competitive advantage. He works with you to customize *The 12 Pillars of Peak Performance* to help your program maximize your athletes' potential. There are a limited number of slots available each year.

Get started by visiting
BrianCain.com/Consulting

1-ON-1 COACHING

Cain works one-on-one with athletes and coaches of all levels. He is now offering one-on-one coaching opportunities where he can work with you directly to apply the information in this manual to your life so that you can compete at the highest level and win the game of your life. This is the **most exclusive access** to Cain and there are a limited number of spots available.

Get started today by visiting
BrianCain.com/Coaching

30985720R10100

Made in the USA
San Bernardino, CA
28 February 2016